PLEASE HELP US TO PROTECT B̶O̶...

A few words about walking and access on Bodmi̶
Bodmin Moor that are unfenced and known as comm̶
may walk anywhere we wish. The "common" in co̶
certain farmers to graze their animals upon these area̶s
not all, of Bodmin Moor is in private ownership, whic̶
should be sought before walking across it. We must k̶   ..ay and
remember that a permissive path is just that – a route fc̶   ᵖᵉ..ᵐˢˢⁱᵒⁿ has been given
for you to walk on a temporary basis and which may be closed should circumstances
change and the landowner wishes to do so.

Please adhere to the countryside code:

- **Be safe – plan ahead and follow any signs**

- **Leave gates and property as you find them**

- **Protect plants and animals and take your litter home**

- **Keep dogs under close control**

- **Consider other people**

A fully explained version of the newly revised countryside code can be found on **www.countrysideaccess.gov.uk,** email **openaccess@countryside.gov.uk** or telephone 0845 100 3298.

Busy traffic on small country roads can be unpleasant and dangerous to all – so slow down and, where possible, leave your vehicle at home, consider sharing lifts and use alternatives such as public transport or cycling.

For public transport information, phone Traveline on 0870 608 2608 or visit **www.countrysideaccess.gov.uk** for useful links.

I sincerely hope you will enjoy this latest book of short walks on Bodmin Moor. If this or either of the other two books in the series, have succeeded in whetting your appetite, then you may be interested to learn that we are developing a further route designed to be more of a challenge; a complete circumnavigation of the moor – 60 miles or more.

Details, such as where you can find a copy of the guidebook and accommodation en route can be found on **www.bobm.info**.

The Best of Bodmin Moor

Six Walks On and Around Bodmin Moor Volume 3

Welcome to the third book of walks published by The Best of Bodmin Moor. The aim of these books is to introduce people to each of the 18 parishes that make up Bodmin Moor. This book contains the last six parishes and includes walks from popular destinations such as Minions and Bolventor and also ones in lesser known areas like Davidstow and St.Tudy.

Once again all the walks are on public rights of way, be it footpaths, bridleways or tarmac roads. This provided me with a challenge in the parish of Davidstow where no one ever walks the footpaths and they have been, for no sense and purpose, abandoned. The walk published in this book is legal but don't expect any signs. Because of this I would advise taking a copy of the OS map for Bodmin Moor (Explorer 109) on all your walks (For the Davidstow walk you will need Explorer 111). Each walk does come with its own map but they are not to scale and only show basic information.

In the summer of 2005 many areas of the moor will be opened to walkers under the CRoW Act. Until then please be aware that even though there is no fence or hedge, all moorland belongs to someone and in theory you are trespassing if you leave the right of way. Please leave all gates as you find them, take all your litter home and don't go climbing over walls.

You may on your walks come across animals, especially in the parishes on the edge of the moor. Bullocks, in particular, are very inquisitive creatures and have a habit of following you through their field. If you run they will chase you, don't worry, turn around and face them, usually they will back off. The only word of warning I have is if you have small dogs, I would advise you to pick them up and carry them if cattle approach, just to be on the safe side. Also I think it goes without saying that dogs should be kept on a lead in any area where farm animals are present.

Please, where possible try to support the local businesses. On several of these walks it is too late and the village post office or shop has already closed, but others remain and rely heavily on passing trade. I have also made note of where bus services can take you to the start of the walk. For the walks on the west side of the moor it may be worth contacting Corlink (0845 850 5556). This is a service that acts like a taxi but charges bus fares.

To enjoy the walks, prepare yourself beforehand. Dress for the terrain and weather, give yourselves enough time to do the walk (I allow 2 mph when walking in Cornwall), and always take a snack and a drink.

Enjoy your walking

Mark Camp

SIX WALKS ON AND AROUND BODMIN MOOR

All walks are graded with stars,
✮ for an easy walk
✮✮✮✮✮ for a strenuous walk.

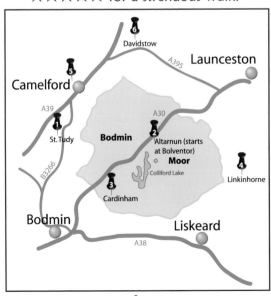

The Four Rectorys Walk
St Tudy

Start of walk	St Tudy Church, Grid Ref SX066764
To get there	St Tudy lies between the A39 and the B3266 Bodmin to Camelford road. Five different lanes lead into the village from all points of the compass.
Services	There is a good village Post Office and stores, The Cornish Arms serves refreshments and food. There are public toilets in Redvale Road. The CORLINK service can be used by those without private transport, for details phone 0845 850 5556
The Walk	Distance 2½ miles ☆☆

The pretty village of St Tudy sits quietly between two of North Cornwall's main commuter roads, The A39 which runs through Wadebridge and on up towards Bude and into Devon runs to the northwest, whilst to the east the B3266 is used by those going from Bodmin to Camelford, or vice versa. All of this movement has little effect on St. Tudy and even though parts of this walk are on public roads the chance of meeting traffic is slim.

The Parish Church of St Tudy & Memorial

The walk starts by the war memorial, standing as it does just inside the churchyard. It is not the only war memorial in the village, the horse chestnut tree to the left is also considered to have that honour. The story goes that it was grown from a conker brought back by a soldier from the battlefield at Flanders in 1915.

The building to the right is called the Clink, built in the 1600's, it has been used for many different roles over the years, from ale house to gaol house. It was also the village school at one time, the chemist and the  doctor's surgery. Today it is used as a centre for the community to meet; the upstairs is used by the Royal Ancient Order of Buffaloes.

Go past the Clink and continue round to the left. After passing the toilets look for a footpath on the other side of the road. This goes down beside Churchtown Farm and can be very muddy at the start. At the far end of the field a stile takes you into another field, head downhill to another stile before views start to open out into the valley below.

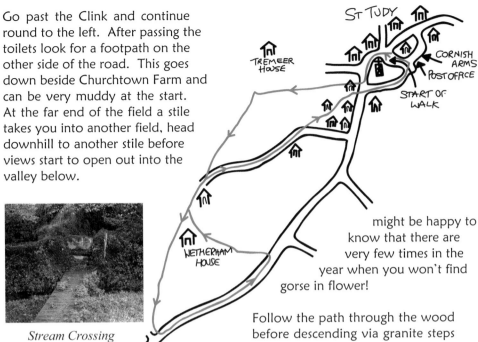

Stream Crossing

From this point and keeping to the left the descent gets steeper as you plunge down to the stream which is crossed by a walkway. Once over this a slate stile has to be negotiated before climbing to a meeting of paths. Turning left, the footpath passes below an old quarry now full of rubbish. Follow the hedge towards the woodland further down the valley.

Once through the gate and into the woods, gorse bushes tower over you. Years ago they would have been cut down and used as fuel. Known in Cornwall as furze, gorse gives off incredible heat and was a favourite in bread ovens. It is also said that when gorse is in bloom, kissing is in season. Down in Cornwall both common and western gorse grow together and both flower at different times of the year. The amorous walkers amongst you

might be happy to know that there are very few times in the year when you won't find gorse in flower!

Follow the path through the wood before descending via granite steps onto a track. Here turn right and follow the track behind Wetherham Lodge. With the Wetherham Woods to your right continue along the side of the valley until the path forks, here take the higher path climbing into the woods for a while before descending behind Wetherham House. This large imposing building was supposedly built in the 1600's and became the village's second rectory. From what I could see of the house through a framework of scaffolding covering at the time of writing, it doesn't look very 17th Century to me. The St Tudy Church guide is not very clear on the matter either, quoting a note written by the Rector of 1854 saying how Alice Reskymer had presented Wetherham to the benefice in 1719. Alice Reskymer had died in 1563 and as far as is known nobody of that name ever owned the house.

Brimstone

A better view of the house will be seen from the front later on in the walk but for now carry on along the valley passing another old quarry (full of bluebells in the spring) and descend to a bridge over the stream. Here you will also find a stile that requires the top bar to be lifted before going over. Turn right and then left across field to where a set of large gates lead out onto the road. The stile 25 yards to the left of the gates is the official route out of the field. Turn left uphill.

Cut into the rock, this lane is typical of many in Cornwall. In spring and early

Wetherham Dovecote

summer it is a mass of pennywort, its spike of pale flowers emerging from spongy round leaves which have mild antiseptic qualities. Shortly you pass a new drive on the left side and a little further on a gate leads into the same field. Although not signposted, the footpath cuts across here to a stile in the fence and then into the pine trees.

Hidden at the top of a slope within the woods is a stile. Once found follow the old path as it runs down to the front of Wetherham House where its full glory should now be revealed. The gardens with dovecote and ornamental lake were open to the public for a short time a few years ago, whether they will be again in the future is unclear at the present time.

A footbridge now has to be crossed and then the drives to both houses, before heading up the old lane into the woods to join the path we walked earlier. Continue back up the valley passing Wetherham Lodge and ignoring the stile back into the woods. Instead continue on the tarmacked lane turning left up the hill.

A mixture of large modern houses and old farm buildings line the lane as it climbs back up towards the village. When a right hand bend is reached go over the stile directly ahead, this takes you along a narrow path between gardens to another stile. To your left is the drive to the latest St Tudy Rectory built in the last few years. The footpath continues between the Glebe sheltered housing bungalows with their tidy

Piggy House

6

gardens and emerges out onto the playing field. The footpath then continues to the other side of the playground along a short alleyway leading out onto the road. To view the third St Tudy Rectory turn right and walk a few yards. It is now a guest house and with nine bedrooms you can understand why the church no longer required it.

Turn round and head back up Redvale Road turning right just before the school. This lane is known as either School Street or Duck Street and leads around the churchyard to come out in the centre of

or just a snack. It is also the place to go if you wish to read more about the village, a notice board outside gives information whilst inside copies of "The Binding Stone, Memories of St Tudy 1900-2000" can be bought. The Binding Stone refers to the circle of stone inset in the ground outside the old blacksmiths shop which is opposite the church. The building was gutted by fire in 2002 but has been rebuilt again to provide a centrepiece to the village. Across the road from it is Garlands, now a private house but originally built as the first Rectory in the village. It must be one of the only houses in the UK to be named after a former headmaster.

The walk is now over and you are once again under the spreading chestnut tree. I have yet to mention the church, or St Tudy's most famous resident, William Bligh. I will leave you to discover the church yourselves, and if you splash out on a copy of the church guide you will gain some information on the Bligh family and much more besides.

The Binding Stone & Village Pump

the village. The quaint little "Piggy House" stands on the left whilst to the right is the wonderfully named "Spare Hill House" with an unusual oval window tucked away round the left side.

Up the lane ahead of you is the "Cornish Arms", perfect for a drink at the end of the walk, whilst the Post Office just before it can provide for those not wanting anything too strong

Orange Tip

To Venture Forth
Bolventor

Start of walk	Jamaica Inn, Bolventor Grid Ref SX184767
To get there	Jamaica Inn lies just off the A30, it can also be reached by driving up the Draynes Valley from Golitha Falls near St Cleer.
Services	Jamaica Inn offers food, drink, has a gift shop and accommodation. There are no other services on the walk.
The Walk	Distance 5 Miles ✫✫✫

A parish is an area of land surrounding a church that in the past controlled much of what went on in the area. Altarnun, of which Bolventor is part, is the largest in Cornwall. This may have something to do with the fact that much of it is wild moorland. When the "modern" parish was defined back in the 12th century there seems to have been an attempt to share out the good and bad land as fairly as possible. Because of this, up on the moor we find large parishes while in the greener lands to the south, parishes are smaller.

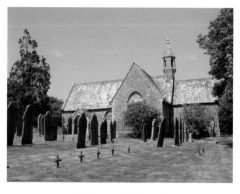

Bolventor Church

Being such a big parish gave me great scope for a walk. Should it be one around the heart of the parish, the village itself with its famous church and Holy well or should it be towards Trewint where John Wesley stopped on his way to spread the word of Methodism? Or should I forsake both religions and head for the open moor.

In the end you could say I even abandoned the parish, for the hamlet of Bolventor was a separate entity for around 150 years after Squire Rodd of Trebartha (North Hill walk Vol 1) tried to create a community there in the mid 1800s. Even the name originates from this time, Bolventor deriving from "bold venture". Rodd had the idea of leasing off large plots of land he owned on the windswept moor with the promises of a new community. No doubt he did very well out of it, but for the tenants life was hard. To entice them he built a church and school but as history has shown even that could not sustain the parish.

The walk starts at what is Bolventor's success story, Jamaica Inn. It was here long before Rodd arrived but in reality has only been a place to visit since the book of the same name was written by Daphne Du Maurier. We will leave our visit until the end of the walk.

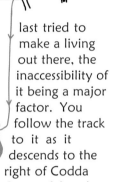

Damsel Fly

Head away from the inn by turning left down the road towards Launceston, this soon bears left under the A30 before curving round to join the main road. Your route is much quieter and follows the lane towards Codda and Bolventor Church. The latter can be reached by turning left a short distance from the junction. The church is now boarded up with plans for a visitor centre in the pipeline.

last tried to make a living out there, the inaccessibility of it being a major factor. You follow the track to it as it descends to the right of Codda farmhouse to a ford. Be careful as the surface of the track is very uneven with loose rocks just waiting to catch the unwary walker. The ford crosses the River Fowey, still in its infancy but already too deep to cross without getting wet, fear not,

Instead, continue along the road to Codda which runs beneath Tolborough Tor to a gate where the tarmac runs out. Ahead of you in the distance can be seen the lonely and abandoned Leskernick farmhouse, nestling under the hill of the same name. It is over 40 years since man

Carneglos Bridge

there is a narrow footbridge to the right. Once over the bridge go through the gate and climb the track to the top of the hill. At the top an open area gives good views all around. In every direction rounded barren hills line the skyline, from Brown Gelly in the south to Leskernick in the north.

Leskernic Farmhouse

9

From here the path descends between fragrant yellow flowered gorse bushes. In places it is little more than a washed out gulley and it may be easier to take the higher ground just to the left of the path. Immediately upon reaching the bottom, the path goes through a gate into a field on the right, head for the fingerpost ahead of you then turn right. Do not try to cut the corner as you could end up further "in to" Bodmin Moor than you planned. As it is, the far end of the field where a gate leads into another field can be very soggy at times. The path now runs along the bottom edge of the field until a clapper bridge is reached over a dried up watercourse. Turn left here and head uphill following the signs. They lead you into a cutting strewn with loose rock; this is all that remains of Tresellyn Tin Mine. A document written in 1876 quotes the Earl of St Germans, Squire Rodd of Trebartha and Augustus Coryton of Pentillie nr Saltash as being involved in the mine, but I could find no other record of its existence.

As you leave the jumble of rocks an entrance into the hillside appears, it is open to all but DO NOT ENTER, I have no idea how far it goes in or how safe it is. The footpath turns right again at the top of the field going through a gate. The OS map shows the footpath going towards the farmhouse but this route apparently no longer exists; instead follow the fingerpost heading left uphill across the field to wooden gates. This joins up with an old track which goes off to the right and then follows a wall above Trezelland farm. When the wall turns sharp right continue across the rough moorland to the gateway in the fence running alongside the track to the farm. Cross the track and continue in a similar direction down through the gorse until you come to a stile over the hedge, do not cross this stile but instead follow the hedge (and the fingerpost sign, to the left) until you reach the top corner of a field on your right. The fingerpost here had been uprooted when I walked the route and there was no definite path visible. As far as I can make out the path goes uphill diagonally to the left crossing an open area strewn with "islands" of granite. At some point you should see the mobile phone mast behind the house at Cannaframe, head towards this and you should find a gateway with a footpath signpost. Another field is crossed and you once again reach the farm track, turn right.

An unwelcome detour has to be made now in order to cross the A30. This involves heading east to reach a tunnel under the main road and then doubling back down the other side. You are now on the old A30, notice the difference. Bolventor was bypassed in the early 1990's and now vehicles sail past not even noticing. The old road climbed and dipped its way from Launceston and in many places had no room for

Stunted Woodland

overtaking, pity the poor traveller stuck behind a tractor.

At the end of the road (and it does end) take the footpath out across the fields to your left. You now have to cross several fields walking in the general direction of Brown Gelly – the rounded hill in the distance with a bump (barrow) on top. After crossing a dry gulley you enter a field dotted with gorse bushes, try to proceed in the same direction as you descend. If you get it right you should arrive at a stone stile in the hedge about 100 meters up from the bottom of the field. Cross this and keep to the top edge of the field until signposts point you right to a bridge over the Fowey River.

After the hustle and bustle of the A30 this is a wonderful peaceful retreat. Whilst I was there iridescent damselflies darted upstream whilst a buzzard flew silently amongst the lichen covered trees. This is one of those places you feel you don't want to tell people about, so keep it to yourselves and let it be our little secret.

Even the old path that climbs up the other side of the bridge is magical and you wonder what history it holds. On the left the woods fall away to the river and the beginning of what is known as Draynes Valley. In the 1970's there was talk of flooding the valley to create a reservoir. Thankfully this never happened, the planners deciding on what is now Colliford Lake reservoir over to the west. As you reach the top of the track the views open out down the valley with Brown Gelly once again prominent to the right.

Reaching the farm a narrow footpath keeps you separated from the animals

Small Copper

and once out into the yard follow the track down to the road. Turn right here and climb up towards Bolventor, the road can be busy so keep an eye and ear open to traffic. Good views soon open out to the north and you should be able to pick out most of the route you have walked between here and Leskernick.

As you enter Bolventor you pass the old school on the left, this closed down several years ago when the number of children in the area became so low it could not be sustained. A little further on we once again reach the old A30 and across the road Jamaica Inn. No longer the "dark and rambling place with long passages and unexpected rooms" that Mary Yellan was forced to move to in the book, it is now a modern tourist attraction geared up for coach loads of visitors throughout the year. The room where she slept is still over the doorway and the spot where Joss Merlyn was found dead can still be seen inside.

If you haven't read the book I recommend you do so, it is full of images of the moor and a life long forgotten. The moor was a wild place then, a place never visited by outsiders. Nowadays the A30 takes many thousands of people across the moor, but how many of them stop, get out of the car and walk out to where the fields end and the wildness still resides? With the help of this book and the previous two I hope you have enjoyed it and will continue to explore further over the years.

The Other Cardinham Walk
Cardinham

Start of walk	Cardinham Church, park outside village hall. Grid Ref SX124687
To get there	Three roads leave the A30 north of Bodmin and head towards the Church. Cardinham can also be reached from the A38 Liskeard/Bodmin road.
Services	There are no services in the village.
The Walk	Distance 3 Miles ✯✯

St Meubreds Chuch..........

Cardinham is another of those Cornish parishes that has no real centre of population.   The few houses dotted around the church and also the little community of Millpool to the north being the only "built up" areas.   Elsewhere the countryside is dotted with smallholdings and farms situated between high moorland and wooded valleys. For many people it is these wooded valleys for which Cardinham is best known, providing as they do, easily accessible recreation areas. The walk that follows includes its own little woodland valley but one far removed from the coniferous plantations found elsewhere.

The walk starts at the 15th century church, built on a site dedicated to St Meubred in 1085. He was said to be a 5th century hermit and information in the church states that he was beheaded in Rome. This is backed up by a window in St Neot church that shows him carrying his head. It is thought that he is buried here in the churchyard, although the shrine dedicated to him has long disappeared. The only thing remaining from those dark times is the base of the cross at the top of the steps. It is thought to date from Roman times although the cross atop of it is dated at 900AD. A finer and older cross is to be found just outside the porch, this one dates

.... and Cross

12

back to 800AD and the markings on its shaft are thought to be Scandinavian in origin.

A look around the inside of the church is worthwhile before starting the walk, but once done proceed down the

The Glynn Memorial

steps back to the road and head up the lane straight across. The lane bends round to the left to where old

Treselea Cross

farm buildings have been redeveloped into housing. Take the footpath that goes between the buildings and into a field used as a small camp site. At the top end a gate on the left hand side lets you into the next field. Keeping to the hedge you will come to a metal gate leading into a larger field, go through this and then through the gate immediately on the left. Walk diagonally across this field towards the houses at the top, just below them there is a stile leading out into the road.

Turn right here and walk up the road to Treslea Cross, here another ancient cross marks the road junction. There are said to be at least six crosses in Cardinham parish, including the two at the church. Most were put up in the 9th and 10th centuries as waymarks across the wild moor, before the land was enclosed and cultivated. (For more crosses see the Camelford walk).

13

Leave the road here and climb the steps up the hedge opposite. These steps are granite slabs set into the hedge and require some agility to scale! Once over, follow the hedge on your right hand side to a gate into an old lane, go through this and over steps and a stile to the right. Note that below the steps a passageway runs through the wall, I am sure this is now used by badgers who frequent the area, but it may have originally been built to allow water to pass through. As you enter the field on your left you will notice a dry ditch or "leat" that runs across the field. At one time this was full of water flowing off the high moor to the village below; we will now use it to guide us onwards.

The leat runs across the next three fields bordered in places by large granite boulders. In the last field slabs have been used to build an old clapper bridge, now obsolete. From here good views can be had of Treslea Downs to the right and beyond into east Cornwall. These end when the path enters woodland and turns right downhill. In the spring this whole area is covered in bluebells whilst autumn

brings a wonderful carpet of gold and red leaves. At the bottom, the ford marked on OS maps has disappeared to be replaced by a bridge, turn left and

Cutting out a granite lintel ...... but not this time

follow the road uphill with the river running through a mini gorge on your right. The lane leaves the woods after a while and continues climbing. As it levels off a footpath goes off to the left signposted by a yellow arrow. Do not go through gate but take the path to the right of the gate.

The most frequent users of this path are badgers, though you will be very lucky to see them. What you will see are their large setts, in fact you cannot miss them, as you have to walk over them. At the top of the path you enter a field with a large earthwork on your left; this is Bury Castle, an Iron Age hill-fort. During the 1000 years before the birth of Christ the climate had become pretty inhospitable on Bodmin Moor and much of it was only populated during the summer months by farmers who moved back down to lower ground during the winter, a practice known as transhumance.

The people of the moor moved to the edges where deep wooded valleys gave shelter and land could be more easily farmed. To protect themselves they built forts on high ground, Bury Castle being one such example. Allabury, which featured in the North Hill walk in Book 1, is another.

The footpath goes around the hill-fort anticlockwise passing an outer bank. Aerial photography suggests there was another defensive bank further out again. Great views can be had from up here; you would have no problem seeing your enemies approaching. A gate leads into another field where views of the village can be had as you

Aerial View of Bury Castle.

Photo: Steve Hartgroves, Cornwall Historical Environment Team

head downhill to a stile beside a gate on the right of the field. Go over the stile and turn right to another gate onto the Moor. Bear left through the gorse until you reach a signpost that points you left downhill over another disused watercourse.

The footpath carries on down until you reach a silage clamp on your left, and goes below it, joining a track that takes you to down to the road from Mount to Millpool. At the road turn left and then right down another track. You will soon reach the old farm buildings at Penpoll, please make sure any gates you go through are left as you find them.

Once you reach the road again turn right and descend to the village where you pass the school. Built in 1882 to replace an earlier school near the church, it is now the centre of a community that has no shop or pub. Those two services were once to be found up near the church to which we will return by turning left at the crossroads. As the road climbs gently, the cottages in front of the church were once the Volunteer Inn and the Post Office respectively. Sadly if you now wish to finish the walk with a drink you will have to drive to The London Inn at St. Neot or The Blisland Inn at Blisland, both of which serve excellent snacks and meals.

Holly Blue

15

The Mines and Mills Walk
Linkinhorne

Start of walk	Old Station car park, Minions. Grid Ref SX263714
To get there	Minions lies north of Liskeard and can be reached a variety of ways. The B3254 from Liskeard to Launceston is possibly the best route turning off at Upton Cross. If coming from the west, leave the A38 at Dobwalls or the A30 at Bolventor.
Services	Minions is well served with two tea shops, a pub and a Post Office / general stores. Rilla Mill also has shops and a pub. There are public toilets in Minions. At the time of writing there are no bus services in the area.
The Walk	Distance 9 Miles ★★★★★ (can be broken into two separate shorter walks).

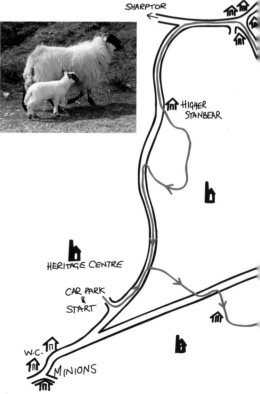

This walk takes place in and around the main mining area of Bodmin Moor, an area that would have been very sparsely populated up until the mid 1800's. Before then the village of Minions did not exist and the parish's centre was far to the east. Before we head in that direction take a look around you. You are surrounded by the remains of man's desire to seek out what riches lie deep underground.

The car park is very near the site of the old Rillaton depot of the Liskeard Caradon Railway, built in 1844 to transfer minerals down towards Looe. The ruined

Minions Heritage Centre

16

engine houses of Wheal Jenkins sit across the road under Caradon Hill whilst to your north the former Houseman's engine house now contains the Minions Heritage Centre.

Let us now start the walk by heading away from the village by turning left out of the car park and along the road towards Henwood and Sharp Tor. In front of you is the engine house of the Prince of Wales mine, a late addition to the industrial landscape and one which you may visit towards the end of the walk. For now you must find a stile on the right hand side of the road, clearly marked with a footpath sign, by keeping to the left hand side of the field another stile is reached. In the field to your left is a large open shaft safely fenced off from curious onlookers. Cross the next field diagonally to the right, over a stile and through another couple of small fields to the road. Be careful

as you cross the road and turn left down it for a short stretch. Another footpath is soon reached on the right taking you downhill to a gate which leads onto open moorland.

The next stretch of the walk takes you down the valley past numerous stream works, small water powered processing systems designed to extract tin or copper from the waste the larger mines threw away. All around you are bumps and hollows, wheel pits and buddles. A buddle is a circular pit where sediment settled, separating the minerals from the mud, you walk right through one as you turn left over the small clapper bridge.

Continue on down the valley following the yellow arrows on the waymarked

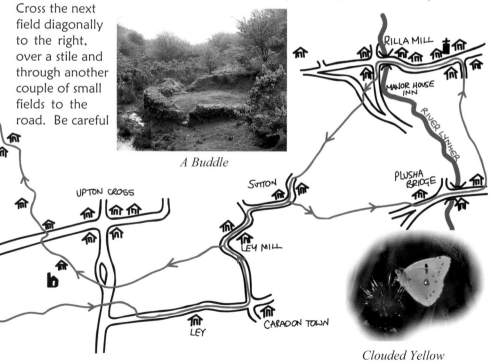

A Buddle

Clouded Yellow

posts. Most of the industrial history is hidden to all but the most knowledgeable but eventually you will come across the Marke Valley complex of mines. This overgrown mine started life in the late 1830's but the remains that can be seen today date from the 1850's. Although a lot of copper and some tin was mined here, its quality was not great and by 1890 the mine had closed. All the buildings are in a very bad state of repair and the shaft is open. Please stick to the footpath and do not be tempted to explore the area.

Shortly the path leaves the moor and after running alongside a row of oak trees follows an old narrow lane to the road. Cross here with care and then manoeuvre yourself through/over the stile into the field. Cross this diagonally towards the red roofed barn full of old farm machinery. A track here leads once again to a road, but to reach it you will have to work out how to open and close several gates, and avoid an electric fence.

Turn left down the lane and onto Ley where the old farm house on the right contradicts the modern building on the left. Spring flowers thrive here in the lane as it gently descends to Caradon Town where you are greeted by dogs, ducks and peacocks. Beside the pond on the right is the old pump and covered well dedicated to St John. In the past they probably served quite a large community, it is thought that the farm here once belonged to Launceston Priory and a monk's ghost is still said to haunt the area. Turn left here and ascend the hill with views opening up through gateways left and right. Early purple orchids, bluebells and pink campion add colour in the late spring sunshine as you descend towards Ley Mill. It is here that the walk can be shortened by turning left upstream towards Marke Valley. ***To follow this route jump to*** ☆

Ley Mill takes its name from a mill that once sat on the south side of the valley, nothing remains, and so it is best to head on slowly up the steep hill cut out of the rock, taking the first lane on the right towards Sutton. This hamlet is in the process of being renovated and most of the old farm building are being repointed and tided up. Turn right in front of "The Grange". The footpath crosses a stile into a small orchard then over another stile onto a rough track which descends steeply into the valley. At the bottom, a fingerpost directs you to a path between the stream and a reed filled pond. Follow this for a short distance before crossing another stile and then over a footbridge into a field. Turning left don't do as I did and head for the gate, the route is further up the field where a stile takes you into another field. This one is crossed above the gorse covered slopes to a set of

Caradon Town Pump & Well

steps over a hedge. This is a good place to sit and rest, the views behind you are of high moor whilst in front of you they are of green fields.

From here it is downhill along the edge of a couple of fields to the road (if you are using the OS Explorer 109 map, it's just run out!) Turn left in front of the cottage towards Rilla Mill and Linkinhorne. Don't take next turning to Rilla Mill but continue on past the old forge and over Plushabridge. This is the River Lynher, which we last crossed in book 1 on the North Hill Walk. Go up the hill and once past two cottages on the left turn onto a footpath that goes along a grass track to a stile that will challenge anybody who suffers from vertigo. Once over this follow the line of oak trees across the field to another stile hidden under a holly tree. In the next field contour round the field to steep steps beside a gate in the distant corner (not the gate at the top), then sharp left over a footbridge.

Keep to the right hand hedge as you climb up with good views of Sharp Tor, Stowe's Hill and Caradon to your left. A gate leads into a lane on the outskirts of Rilla Mill, continue along it to the road then turn left downhill past the large Methodist Church. Like Ley Mill, Rilla Mill gets its name form the fact that the manorial mill was here. Rillaton Manor was mentioned in the Domesday Book as Redleston, the "town by the ford". Nowadays a well built bridge takes you over the river, on your way down to which you pass the Manor House pub and restaurant.

Once over the bridge turn left just after the Post Office. After a short distance

turn right up steps to a stile. A short sharp climb through a meadow, full of wood anemones in the spring, brings you out onto a road where you turn left again before another set of steps on your right takes you into a field. The footpath from here goes straight across the next three fields. At the time I walked it the farmer had made no attempt to keep the legal way clear of crops and I had to walk through them, hopefully things will have changed by the time this is published. After the third field is crossed, a nice signpost points diagonally towards Sutton. Cross the field and enter an old lane passing through three sets of gates before you reach the road.

Turning left this next stretch to Ley Mill retraces the route taken earlier down to the river. ⭐ ***Those who opted for the shorter walk should rejoin the text here.***

Turn right upstream signposted to Marke Valley, this path is well signposted and after a short stretch across open ground enters Leymill Wood.

Marke Valley Boundary Stone

You are once again entering mining country, this being the eastern and earlier part of the Marke Valley complex. Soon after entering the wood follow the upper waymarked route, but at the second fork you should take the lower route, you will pass an open adit on your left. An adit is a drainage tunnel for the mine and because of this is usually flooded, DO NOT ENTER. A little further on, and just after passing the remains of a wheelpit below to your right, the path zig zags up steps to the main road.

Cross the road and descend down the old road for a short stretch. Turning left down a track brings you to a metal gate, go through this and follow the track below the waste tips of Marke Valley mine. The wall running along on your left is constructed of blocks of iron rich mine waste. The path leads to a run down assortment of sheds where it picks its way between them before reaching a tarmac'd area. Here you should turn right in front of the house to where the footpath climbs up

Past its best

around a boundary fence. Keep an eye out for a rather large dog which has a habit of escaping. At the top of the woods sits an old Fordson tractor, long retired. Go over the stile and follow the hedge round to the left, eventually bringing you to the road.

This is the road from Upton Cross to Minions and anyone wanting to shorten the walk could turn left here and proceed carefully (along what is

quite a busy lane), back to the start. For those still "up for it" turn right. After a short distance a lane leads off on the left between houses, take this. Follow the concrete path until a sign points right towards Knowle Farm and the Cornish Cheese Co. Pass around the farmyard and follow the lane out across the fields, the village of Henwood soon coming into view nestling below Sharptor. The tor directly in front is Notter Tor.

Passing the Cornish Cheese Co buildings on your right continue along the tarmac track to the end, here a gate on your right leads into a field. Cut straight across the field in the direction of Henwood keeping to the right of the large tree on the edge of the wood. Soon you will come across a redundant stile leading into the woods on your left, go over it if you wish and descend down to the stream where a footbridge saves you getting your feet wet. All along the valley floor are the remains of the Darley Slime works, a late 1800's processing area for the extracting of minerals from the waste products of Phoenix Mines on the hill above. A large wall to your left is a fine example of other remains beyond it.

Exit the wood and once over a stile continue up through a field dotted with large boulders. Another stile at the top leads into another field and then another before the road is reached. Turn left here and climb up to Henwood where a bench in the centre of the village makes a fine resting point. It is easy to forget as you sit here in the peace and quiet of the Cornish countryside that 150 years ago this village was at the centre of the industrial revolution. Up to 12 engine houses belched smoke from the hillside opposite, machinery toiled all day, clanking and banging, and disease was rife in what would have been little more than a shanty town. To get an idea of what life was like up here, read "Catch the Wind" by EV Thompson, a novel that tells of the trials and tribulations of a miner's life.

Sharptor

Leave the village heading in a westerly direction uphill towards Minions, a road soon branches off to Sharptor (a lovely walk, but not today).

Head downhill for a short distance before the road once again climbs between trees. Half way up stop and turn round, Sharptor towers above you belying its quite lowly height of 378 meters (1209 ft). Continue uphill to the cottages at Stanbear where a new bridleway drops off on the left, follow this down to a footbridge. You are now at the top of the Darley Slime works and on your right is the wall of the large reservoir which collected the water to power the wheels used to drive the machinery. Now breached, only a shallow pond hides behind the wall, still fed from adits further up the valley.

Follow the wall around to the right to where the path climbs up onto the former Phoenix mine site. Little remains to the untrained eye of what was the largest mine in the area except for the odd pile of masonry covered in cotoneaster. The lower part, rich in heathers, gorse and rhododendron bushes contrasts heavily with the barren wasteland you reach at the top. Here nothing grows on the mineral rich waste tips where amateur geologists can sometimes be seen hunting for treasures. At the top of the barren area the path divides in front of a fenced off shaft. Turn right and follow the signposts down into the valley. The path soon climbs again curving round between shafts to reach the road beside the remains of Hamilton's pumping engine house. Turn left here and follow the road back to Minions.

Over to your left you can see the remains of the Prince of Wales mine. This was built in 1907 to tap into the by then closed down Phoenix mine. Although much money was spent on building the mine, no ore of any value was brought out and by 1914 it had closed never to reopen. Over the last 10 years or so the buildings, which are on private land, have been tidied up and made safe.

On returning to Minions you will find a choice of places to refresh yourselves if needed, plus public toilets close to the road. There are many other fine walks to be done from the village, to visit either industrial sites or prehistoric ones. At the time of writing (Oct. 2004) many are still only accessible by the fact that the landowners do not mind people walking on their land, please respect their generosity.

The Crooked River Walk
Camelford

Start of walk	Bridge Car park, North end of Camelford. Grid Ref SX108838
To get there	Camelford lies on the A39, North Cornwall trunk road.
Services	All services canbe found in the town. Public toilets are near to the start of the walk in Enfield Park.
The Walk	Distance 4 Miles ★★

The town of Camelford lies just off the northwest edge of the moor and owes its existence to the fact that it was an important crossing point of the River Camel on the old road that ran from the west up to Exeter and beyond. Today the main road, the A39, still trundles through the heart of the town and over the bridge which many years ago replaced the Camel ford. Traffic congestion is now a major problem and plans are afoot to build a bypass to the northwest of the town, more of which later.

The walk starts from the church car park, just above the bridge. The church was built in 1938 and is dedicated to St Thomas of Canterbury. From the outside you could be forgiven for thinking it an older building but once inside the modern style is clear to see. There had been a chapel near this site as far back as the early 1300's but during the reformation it closed down. The ruins remained into the 18th Century when the owner of the Bell Inn opposite used them to store firewood. The bell from which the inn took its name was later hung in the Town Hall and can now be seen beside the entrance to the building.

This walk starts by crossing the road by the church to where the Bell Inn once stood; now turn right towards the town centre. The large buildings on either side of the road date back to the 1700's when Camelford was in its prime and had two members of Parliament. Thomas Pitt, cousin of the Prime

Camelford Church and Bell

22

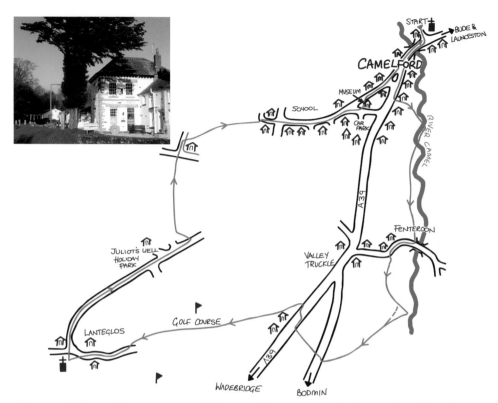

Minister William Pitt, once owned the Manor House on the other side of the road. He was awarded the title Lord Camelford and Baron Boconnoc after the family home near Lostwithiel. Always a bit of a maverick, he died in a duel at the age of 29.

Cross over the River Camel for the first time today and walk past the Mason's Arms, once a coaching inn. The next big building you come to is the Free Methodist Chapel, built in 1837 to serve a group of rebellious Wesleyans who had broken away from the main Methodist group in the town. Today it serves as the centre for all Methodist religion in the area.

You are now in the centre of the town, the former market place. The old town hall takes centre stage, now fulfilling the role of the library. It was built in 1806 by the Duke of Bedford, who at that time owned most of the town. Apart from building the Town Hall and adding the clock tower he also made sure the pavements were in a good state of repair and that the members of Parliament sent by the town were to his approval. The lower Kings Arms Inn was even renamed The Bedford.

The Duke of Bedford eventually lost interest in Camelford and shifted his support to Tavistock. Shortly after, the Earl of Darlington moved in and the inn's name changed once again. Now called the Darlington Hotel, the

building sits beside the road just up from the Town Hall. In 1995 it was gutted by fire but has since been rebuilt in the same style.

The Clock & Camel

As you pass the Darlington Hotel, turn around and look up at the weathervane atop of the Town Hall, it is of a golden camel. Although long associated with the town, the Camel in Camelford has nothing at all to do with the "ship of the desert". It is thought to be a derivation of the Cornish word for "cam" meaning crooked and "allan" meaning beautiful.

Common Blue

Fenteroon Bridge

To join the "beautiful crooked river" you need to turn left under an arch a little further up the road. Once down at the river follow the path to the right, this now takes you down stream via

bridges, kissing gates and stiles to Fenteroon Bridge.

Climb up onto the road via steps in the wall and turn right. The road curves round to the left under Fenteroon farm, built on the site of an earlier manor house. Past the farm entrance the footpath goes off to the left beside a field gate. It is tucked away to the left of the gate and hidden behind the hedge. Once through the gate the footpath runs alongside the field to a stile, where it then goes through the centre of another field enclosed by modern fences. The stiles on this part of the walk are nearly all made of the local slate, be careful if using them when wet as they may be slippery. Once safely over the next stile the path drops down through a beech wood to the water meadow below. Head across the meadow to a large gap between hedges, here the path continues towards the river where a footbridge takes you into Advent parish (see Book 2). You need not go as far as the river but can stay near the right hand side of the field to regain the footpath as it climbs up into the woods beside a particularly large beech tree. Once into the woods the path becomes clear as it follows an old track upwards to the fields. Steps up the side of the wall save you from untying the gate and then by keeping to the bottom of the field you should find another stile in the far corner.

After climbing over this stile again keep to the left hand hedge as you rise steadily towards the road. At the top the stile gives great views behind you out onto the moor. Advent Church can

24

be seen as can the rugged summit of Roughtor. Going down the stile be very careful of the road ahead. This is the B3266 Bodmin to Camelford road and can be busy at times. You need to cross here to a stile on the other side of the road just to the right.

Peacock

you need turns left down the lane just before the big road sign. **PLEASE BE CAREFUL.**

As I mentioned at the start of the walk, there are plans for a bypass around Camelford. If this goes ahead, it will rejoin the original route somewhere around this point. Hopefully it will make walking safer.

A completely new view opens out once on the other side of the road. Directly ahead lies the village of Delabole on the horizon, whilst over to the left Cornish farmland stretches away for miles. Through the middle of it runs the Camel valley, snaking towards Padstow and the sea.

Walk across the field towards the bottom right hand corner where you now reach the A39. Of all the walks in this series of books, this is possibly the most dangerous stretch. Once over the stile you must turn right and walk along the road, just before you get to the bend I would advise you to cross and walk the last few 20 or so yards with the traffic behind you. The footpath

Leaving the road behind, the footpath follows the lane down and past Tramagenna Farm. Steps lead up on the right onto the Bowood Golf Course. Please make sure all dogs are on leads as you cross the course, and look out for golf balls! The route across the links is marked by white posts, the first one of which stands beside the roofless building to your left as you come up the steps.

The Bowood Golf Course has been created on land that during the 13th Century was a Royal deer park belonging to the Black Prince. It is an 18 hole course with a par of 72, for those of you in the know. I must admit to not being a golfing person and my view is that it spoils a good walk. Saying that, most of the golfers I saw on the course were travelling round in buggies and the only walking they did was a gentle stroll to play the ball.

Having negotiated the greens and bunkers the path reaches a lane where if you turn right takes you down to Lanteglos Church. On your right are the grounds of Lanteglos Country House Hotel, formerly the Rectory, an impressive building designed by AW

Lanteglos Church

Exit the churchyard by the War Memorial and take the road opposite, signposted Camelford. Halfway up the hill a lonely bench sits on the left hand side, it has no view to look at and rarely gets a bottom placed on it, feel free to make use of it.

Just a little further on from the golf course is the entrance to Juliot's Well Holiday Park. The well itself sits down in the valley and has no permissible access. A footpath out across the fields leaves from the Bowling Club's car park, the official route going from a stile at the top of the car park down the hedge and out through another stile hidden amongst the trees and shrubs. It is just as easy to walk straight through the car park. The footpath goes straight across the field to go through a gate to the right of a ruined building, from there carrying on towards the nearest house.

Pugin in 1847, he had previously designed the Houses of Parliament at Westminster. The parish church of Lanteglos by Camelford sits here in the valley, over a mile from the centre of the town and surrounded by fields. It must have been a great relief to the parishioners when the new church was built in 1938 near the start of this walk. The church is only open on Wednesday afternoons during the summer months, but if closed it is still worth walking around the churchyard to look at the collection of Celtic stone crosses or just to admire the wildflowers that are allowed to take over in the spring.

Once over the stile, cross the road and look out for an old Celtic cross in the hedge to your left. Until 1984 it was still being used as a gatepost into the field, but after it had been hit a few times by tractors the owners were persuaded to move it. It is unusual in having an incised shield carved into its shaft. A little further up the road an old kissing gate leads into a field on the right. Keeping to the left hand side head for the top corner where another kissing gate/stile provides access. If and when the new bypass goes ahead there will be a footbridge over it at this point.

Lest We Forget

The footpath regains the road in the top left corner of the field. In front of you, behind the modern houses, stands the old Camelford union workhouse. When it was built in 1858 it could house 80 inmates and also had a small isolation hospital beside it. Today it has been divided up into several private houses.

Proceed right, up the road to the crossroads, another cross stands to your right, the head is original, the base modern. This area of Camelford is known as Sportsman's after the inn that used to stand here. It finally closed in 1907 after winning a reprieve in 1884 when the local authority tried to close it down on grounds of hygiene. It must have been in some state as at that time Camelford was called the dirtiest town in Cornwall by the West Briton newspaper.

Cross the road with care and walk down Clease Road with Camelford school on your left. After passing the Penclease

residential home, cross the road to the museum. This is a great place to learn more about the life of the area in the past including farming, quarrying, and general day-to-day living. The building also houses the Tourist Information Centre and an art gallery. It is open from Easter to the end of September.

From the museum, head towards the centre of the town via Chapel Street. On the way down the chapel that gave the street its name is on the left. Both the Methodist Chapel and adjacent Sunday school are now private dwellings. The Town Hall once again comes into view and from here it is a short walk back down the main street to the bridge and the car park. For those seeking refreshments there are the Mason's Arms or the Darlington Hotel plus a couple of cafes. For those that want to walk further, there is Enfield Park down by the bridge where a short explore should take no longer than 20 minutes.

Camelford Museum

The Contractual Obligations Walk
Bogs, blocked paths and barbed wire!
Davidstow

Start of walk	Davidstow Church car park, Grid Ref SX152873
To get there	Davidstow Church is on the A395 about 3 miles northeast of Camelford.
Services	There are no services near this walk
The Walk	Distance 2½ Miles ★★

I left the Davidstow walk till last only because it has gained a reputation during my research for these walks as being a parish without footpaths. They do exist but have been ignored for so long that there are no signposts and are very difficult to follow and walk. However, on a dry morning in November I decided to be brave and venture forth. What follows is a short walk that I would only recommend to keen and agile walkers as it involves crossing several streams and climbing over several gates. Wear your wellies!

Holy Well

The walk starts from the small car park beside the church. A Holy Well is just across the field and is worth a visit although it has no curing powers. It was renovated in the 1870's by a Michael Williams and his initials can be seen carved above the door. Leaving the car park, cross the road and head down the lane towards Inny Vale holiday village, which is soon passed on the left hand side. There is a shop on site that may be open for refreshments. The road soon starts to climb up to the former Davidstow Board School built in 1877. Like the church, the school stands on its own, the parish having no real centre of population only a collection of small hamlets built around farmhouses. The largest of these is Tremail which is shortly reached and featured in the Domesday Book.

Turn right beside the phone box and wander up between the bungalows. Just after passing one called Oxen Combe there is a gate on the right, go through this into the field. Head off

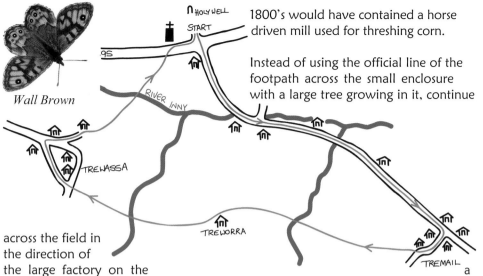

Wall Brown

1800's would have contained a horse driven mill used for threshing corn.

Instead of using the official line of the footpath across the small enclosure with a large tree growing in it, continue across the field in the direction of the large factory on the skyline. This is Dairy Crest's Davidstow Creamery where they produce Cheddar cheese for all the major supermarket chains. On the other side of the field you should find some slate steps taking you up the hedge and into a gorse bush, hidden amongst which you may find some steps leading down the other side. Once safely down head to the far right corner of the next field to where a stile makes life far easier.

Follow the hedge on your right as you descend to a stream. The route of the footpath marked on the OS map would take you straight through the hedge at the bottom and into a dense patch of brambles, to avoid this go left and find somewhere that you can cross the stream without getting wet. The footpath on the other side heads towards the buildings ahead of you, again the route is not clear. Once at the "farm" I turned left around the open barn and then right once on the track beside the buildings. The unusually shaped building on the left is a converted roundhouse, which during the

a short distance up the lane before turning left towards "Belle Tents" and then through the first gate on the right. The entrance to this field was incredibly muddy when I walked the route, you have been warned. Keep to the left side of the field passing through another gate, again very muddy. From here the path descends, again keeping the hedge to your left, towards a marshy area where the sources of the River Inny merge. The Inny could be said to be the unofficial boundary of Bodmin Moor on the northeast side and features in the St Clether walk in Book 1. It eventually joins the meandering River Tamar amongst woodland near Milton Abbot.

Although only a stream at this point it once again causes problems to the walker. The boggy area is best not entered, instead keep to the hedge on your left and once the stream/hedge is reached find a point where it is safe, and accessible, to cross. Even then life is not easy as the other side of the stream is also boggy and similar tactics

29

must be used. If anyone gets through this section with dry feet they have done well!

Once through the mire the path carries on up the field to the left of the buildings. The field gets narrower as it climbs, with good views to the right of the church, whilst over to the left a water treatment plant can be seen in the foreground and the buildings of Davidstow Airfield on the skyline, more of which later.

At the top of the field there is a stile and a gate leading out onto the road, I will let you decide which one is easiest to negotiate! Take the track straight ahead which goes round behind the hamlet of Trewassa. It emerges beside the slate hung former chapel and crosses the road to go down the track opposite. As the track bends to the left to enter a private residence the footpath goes off ahead down a sunken lane. Once again the footpaths of Davidstow live up to their reputation, the gate here is made up of both a modern metal gate and also an ancient wooden one. Neither looked capable of opening and even if they did you are then faced with an impenetrable mass of brambles. My advice is to climb the right side of the gate into the field then follow the route of the footpath as closely as possible. By keeping to the hedge you should come to a stile leading into the corner of the next field. From here the path crosses to another small stile over what is left of the old field boundary and then reaches yet another stream. There is a stile here but it takes some finding, it climbs the bank behind a blackthorn tree after first crossing the

stream. Finally, after this last obstacle has been conquered, it is an easy walk to the gate beside the electricity station and out onto the road. Here turn right and once safe to do so, cross the road to the church.

Considering that there do not appear to be many houses in the parish, it comes as a surprise to find such a large church. Dedicated to St David, the church has been restored on several occasions, the latest

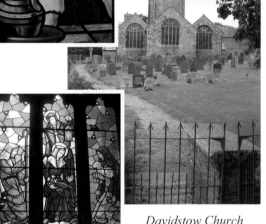

Davidstow Church

being in the 1990s. It is once inside that the full glory of the building is revealed, the stained glass windows totally out of character with the mist prone parish outside. It is also nice to be able to say that the church is always open so not only the windows, but also the carved pew ends can be viewed. One thing I do ask is that if, like mine, your boots are wet and muddy, please remove them before entering.

Charlotte Dymond Memorial

Once inside you find a brief description of the tragic story of Charlotte Dymond whose grave can be found in the churchyard outside, and whose memorial stone is near to Roughtor car park. You may also wish to visit the Shire Hall in Bodmin where there is an entertaining re-enactment of the trial of Matthew Weeks the man "unfairly?" charged with her murder.

Congratulations on doing this walk, it is not easy as I said at the start. If, or when, you do encounter problems on this or any of the walks, please inform the rights of way people at Cornwall County Council. They are there to keep footpaths open and only know of problems when we the walkers tell them. Help them to help us.

RAF Davistow Moor

RAF Davidstow Moor (RAFDM) Airfield was opened in 1942 and became home to 19 Group Coastal Command and was a base for both the RAF and the USAF. Both British Wellingtons and American

Wellington Crew on a Refuelling Stopover

Liberators flew from here as well as many other smaller aircraft. With the airfield lying at just under 1000ft it had a habit of being shrouded in mist and was often unusable, however RAF Davidstow was ideally situated for providing Air Sea Rescue (ASR) services, many returning aircrew owe their lives to the dedication of aircrew on ASR duties. Other operations included maritime reconnaissance, anti-shipping and anti-submarine and as a refuelling base. On May 16th 1944, forty five American Liberators led in by a few Dakotas arrived to be refuelled and rearmed prior to attacking submarine pens at Bordeaux. All aircraft returned safely. The base was also used by the Americans and Canadians for training in the run up to D-Day and was visited by General Eisenhower during 1944. The base ceased operations in 1945 and subsequently fell into disrepair.

Control Tower

Start of the 1.5l Sports Car Race, Whit Monday 1954

The story however does not quite end there because in 1952 it was opened as a motor racing circuit. True to its location, the first meeting was held in torrential rain to a crowd of 3000. Two meetings were held 1953, the first of which was affected by fog (and also delayed until they could clear the sheep from the back straight), and the second suffered from poor crowd attendance as it was a hot sunny day and the crowds went to the beach instead. The two meetings in 1954 were also affected by rain, so for 1955 one race meeting was held on Whit Monday, the 30th May. The highlight of the meeting was a full Formula One race, but racing was never to be held at the track again.

Today the site is derelict; the main Camelford to Altarnun road crosses the bleak expanse and many of the abandoned buildings can still be seen including the old control tower. Many of these buildings are now destined for demolition. The runways, however, are still used for light aircraft. A memorial to all those that served at the base has been erected near the entrance to airfield, close to the creamery site. A small RAF museum is also planned.

More information on the airfield can be found in the book "Memories and Records of RAF Davidstow Moor" by local RAF historian David Keast.

RAF Davidstow Moor Memorial

And finally..........

Well, that's the three books finished. With the help of this book and the previous two, I hope you have enjoyed your walks on Bodmin Moor and will continue to explore further over the years. Once again I would like to thank Kathy for correcting my mistakes and putting up with my muddy boots and smelly socks. Also thanks go out to all the authors whose books, leaflets and websites I have delved into to help with my research, space prevents me from listing them all here. Thanks also to Sally Holden at Camelford TIC, Jeremy Capper for guiding me around Cardinham, Steven Docksey for all those little bits of information that are invaluable and David Keast for additional information on RAF Davidstow Moor.

Last but not least, thanks to all of you who have bought the books and allowed me to go off walking and exploring. I am currently working on a 60 mile complete circumnavigation of the moor which we will publish in 2005.

THE BEST OF BODMIN MOOR

Mark Camp